Secrets of the
QUEENS CLOSET

Secrets of the
QUEENS CLOSET

Simon Bond

Ashford Press Publishing
Southampton
1988

Published by   Ashford Press Publishing 1988
                1 Church Road
                Shedfield
                Hampshire SO3 2HW

British Library Cataloguing in Publication Data

Secrets of the Queen's closet.
    1.   Folk medecine —England—History—
    Sources
    I.   Isitt, Tom
    615.8'82'0942   R487

ISBN 1-85253-045-6

Introduction

We've had this book in our family for years. Called 'The Queen's Closet Opened' it was published in 1655, and is probably the reason I grew up so healthy in mind and body because, in the words of the title page, it contains incomparable secrets in Physick, Chirurgery, Preserving, Candying and Cookery; as they were presented to the Queen by the most Experienced Persons of our Times.' In other words, it's a seventeenth-century alternative medicine book as used by Queen Henrietta Maria, wife of King Charles I, and the royal household.

Whether Queen Henrietta Maria really had anything to do with this book is open to debate, because it was published six years after King Charles was executed and Henrietta Maria had fled abroad. The title page goes on to say that the secrets were 'transcribed from the true copies of Her Majesties own Receipt-Book by W.M. one of her late servants'. In his introduction to the book W. M. claims that he only went public with them to prevent the publication of false copies. He also writes a wonderful disclaimer to the effect that if any of the remedies are altered or corrupted it's the fault of the printer.

Whichever way you look at it, this book is a fascinating insight into the health of seventeenth-century England, and for the benefit of twentieth-century England the time has come to unlock the Secrets of the Queen's Closet.

Seventeenth-century England was not a good place to live. In fact the century wasn't a whole lot of fun wherever you were because Europe was in Big Trouble. After everyone had had such a nice time a century earlier during the Renaissance, Europe was gripped by a destructive backlash, and confusion was the order of the day. Spain was being ruled by Austrians who were having a war with the Dutch, so the Spanish Inquisition moved to Italy and picked on Galileo. The French, meanwhile, had finished massacring the Huguenots and were girding their loins in readiness for the Revolution, while the English, unable to find anyone to fight, declared war on themselves.

To make matters worse, Europe wasn't a healthy place to live anyway. Living conditions in the towns were cramped and squalid, and they weren't much better in rural communities. Personal hygiene was largely unknown, health care almost non-existent, and even if you were lucky enough to make it past childhood it was unlikely that you'd manage your allotted three score years and ten. Black Death, Smallpox, Syphilis, Tuberculosis and Influenza carried off thousands of people every year, so if you made it to middle-age you were doing well. Medical practice was in its formative years and while there was much research being conducted the population relied heavily on 'quack' cures and herbal medicine. Even though the principles of the transmission of infectious diseases was relatively well known as early as 1546, no one fully understood how Bubonic Plague was spread. The line in 'Ring a Ring of Roses': 'atishoo atishoo, we all fall down' derives from the knowledge that the plague was passed on by breathing on other people. However, contemporary cures of the plague were very odd:

'When the sore doth appear then to take a Cock Chick, and pullet, and let the rump be bare, and hold the rump of said Chick to the sore, and it will gape and labour for life and in the end die. Then take another, and a third, and so long as any do die; for when the poison is drawn out the Chick shall live, the sore will presently assuage and the party recover.'

Quite how they imagined applying chicken's bums to their plague boils was going to cure them is beyond comprehension, but believe it they did, and many a chicken must have met an unpleasant end in this way.

To understand just how seventeenth-century Europe came to believe in this sort of quack medicine you have to look at the development of medical practice during the preceeding centuries.

In prehistoric times illness was deemed to be the work of a malevolent spirit and a common cure was trephination – drilling a hole in the top of a patient's skull to let out the evil spirit. Understandably this was rarely beneficial and is doubtless the origin of the phrase 'as much use as a hole in the head'. Nor (perhaps not surprisingly) was the practice of medicine greatly encouraged. In Babylonian times it was decreed that 'if the doctor, in opening an abscess, shall kill the patient, his hands shall be cut off'. I can't see the British Medical Association going much on that. It was also common practice in Babylon to lay the sick out in the street so that passers-by could offer advice...getting a second opinion was dead easy in those days.

It was only during the fifth century BC in Greece that medicine really became a 'science'. Hippocrates (founder of the Hippocratic Oath) subscribed to the theory that health relied on a balance between the four bodily humours: blood, choler, phlegm and melancholy. It was believed in Greek times that most illnesses were caused by excess blood so blood letting and cupping became a common cure for just about anything from a fever to tuberculosis.

Various other discoveries were made by the Greeks but were lost in the 'Dark Ages', locked up in texts which no-one read and studied until universities were invented in the twelfth century. Even then, it was still thought that strange herbs and blood-letting would cure most things. By this time witch-doctors were rather scarce in Europe, so the role of physician was taken over by the clergy who were as ineffectual as everybody else.

The middle ages didn't do a lot for the advancement of clinical medicine, but in an age when everyone's favourite pastime was killing other people military physicians gained a large fund of anatomical knowledge. Amputations were easily performed, sometimes with the benefit of anaesthetics (alcohol), and some patients even survived. In the fourteenth century they found out that a hernia could be operated on without having to remove the reproductive organs as well and they even found that broken limbs could be mended by using weights and pulleys. Cutting for the gall stone became one of the most common operations, but again this had first been performed in Roman times, illustrating how little medicine had advanced in 1400 years.

As if to show just how helpless mediaeval man was, in 1346 Europe succumbed to the worst natural disaster it had ever seen – the Bubonic Plague. In two years, somewhere in the region of two million people perished in Britain – almost half the population in two years. The plague was passed on to humans from rats (a common household pest) via their fleas, and then from person to person in its pneumonic form. In the crowded, walled mediaeval towns the plague spread quickly and thoroughly. There was no cure and no escape.

With the reformation came an inevitable disenchantment with the medical expertise of the clergy (which was precious little to start with) and medical practice passed into the hands of quacks, barber-surgeons and grocer-apothecaries. In those days you could pop down to Vidal Sassoon's for a shave, a bit off the top and sides, and a tooth pulled or a gall stone removed. Then, on your way home, you could stop off at Sainsbury's for two pounds of spuds, a large cabbage and some powdered Unicorn horn or some black tips of crabs' claws. It may have made for one-stop shopping and treatment but medicine wasn't what you'd call an exact science. A quick look at some of the drawings of Leonardo da Vinci will show that artists then had a better working knowledge of anatomy than the hairdressers and grocers at the time. It's hardly surprising, really.

Henry the Eighth, something of an amateur physician himself (his speciality was the surgical removal of his wives' heads), became so worried by the lack of professional ethics being practised in his realm that he passed the first ever Medical Act:

'Physic and Surgery is daily within this Realm exercised by a great multitude of ignorant persons as common artificers, smiths, weavers, and women who boldly and customably take upon them great cures and things of great difficulty in which they partly use scorcery and witchcraft to the grevious hurt, damage, and destruction of many of the King's liege people.'

The act made it an offence to practice medicine unless you were a graduate from a university or had been licensed by a bishop after you'd been examined by a panel of experts.

Not all amateurs were dangerous, however, and the beginning of the sixteenth-century saw several gifted amateurs at work, the most colourful of whom rejoiced in the name of Aureolus Theophrastus Bombastus von Hohenheim 'Paracelsus'. He was the first 'real' physician in that he took absolutely no notice of traditional medical theory, prefering to trust in Chemistry to effect the cure of his patients. He also recognised that goitre and cretinism were related and prescribed mercury as a treatment for syphilis (a particularly popular ailment at the time). In fact, he knew quite a lot about syphilis because he suffered from insanity as a result of the disease and was also known to be partial to excessive drinking. It was quite fitting that he met his end in a tavern brawl at the age of 48.

Another medical rebel of the time was Jacob Nüfer, a Swiss sow-gelder who successfully performed a Caesarean section on his own wife after the doctors had given up all hope of survival for mother and child. No doubt he had enough knowledge of anatomy, an understanding of the necessary hygiene and the right tools to do the operation. Nüfer made such a good job of it that his wife went on to have several other children.

The sixteenth century was when medical research really came of age. All manner of nasty things were observed, diagnosed and cures prescribed (usually to little or no effect, but at least they were trying). But if common or garden cures weren't too successful, the abilities of the surgeons had never been better. A French surgeon by the name of Ambroise Paré was the first person to try anything other than hot oil on the stumps of amputees, and he was also pretty adept at knocking up false limbs, trusses, glass eyes and false teeth carved from ivory.

Just when they thought they were doing so well, a 'sweating sickness' epidemic swept Europe killing people in their thousands. It's thought now that it was a particularly virulent strain of flu from which people had no natural immunity, and not even any aspirin.

At the end of the sixteenth century Johannes Kepler discovered how eyes work and thus why spectacles were beneficial. Up till that point people had been wearing glasses without knowing why, but now Kepler had opened the way for four centuries of opticians to rob us blind with outrageous prices.

Which brings us back to the seventeenth century again. A good century for medical research, a bad one for medical practice and an even worse one for the populace of Britain. It started off quite promisingly with Galileo, Descartes and Sanctorius all busy inventing telescopes, thermometers and doing a lot of thinking all over Europe, while in England a boat load of religious maniacs sailed off in the Mayflower to become Americans. Definitely a good start.

It was downhill all the way from then on, however, because in 1624 there was the first serious outbreak of the plague since 1346. In London alone 41,300 people died of the plague and twelve years later another 10,400 people went the same way. Just when everyone had recovered from the plague, Cromwell started causing trouble for Charles I and in a thoroughly cavalier fashion Charles I declared war on everyone with a round head. Three years of civil war followed during which thousands more perished and which ended when Charles completely lost his head and Parliament was forced to take over the running of the country until they called in the monarchy again in 1660.

While all this was going on, William Harvey lectured to the Royal College of Physicians in the 1620s on his latest discovery – how blood circulates round the body, the workings of the heart and the use of valves in the blood system. Despite demonstrating his findings, most of his contemporaries remained sceptical, a typical reaction of the narrow-minded medical profession of the time.

Robert Boyle published 'The Sceptical Chemist', after the Restoration, which proposed the theory that chemical actions occur between moving particles. He also discovered how lungs work by opening up the chest of an animal and keeping it alive by inserting a pair of bellows into its wind pipe.

The apparent lack of natural disasters at this time must have been a welcome break for the people of England, but it turned out to be the calm before the storm. In 1665 England was struck by another outbreak of the plague, now a perennial favourite of the whole of Europe. In London alone 68,000 people died that year, and at the peak of its popularity the Black Death killed 8000 Londoners a week. It's difficult to imagine what it must have been like living through that – no cure, no escape, just the stench of death all around...and the fear. Councils appointed wardens to check people entering towns, red crosses were drawn on the doors of infected houses and patrolling watchmen were supposed to make sure that no one approached these houses and no one left them. Despite these measures the plague spread at an alarming rate, which is hardly surprising when you read what Samuel Pepys writes in his diary on February 12, 1666:

'Comes Mr Caesar, my boy's lute-master, whom I have not seen since the plague before, but he hath been in Westminster all this while, very well; and tells me, in the height of it, how bold people there were, to go in sport to one another's burials; and in spite too, ill people would breathe in the faces, out of their windows, of well people going by...Ill news this night, that the plague is encreased this week, and in many places else about the town, and at Chatham and elsewhere.'

Contrary to popular belief, the Great Fire of London that raged during the beginning of September 1666 was not responsible for the end of the plague. The fire decimated the City of London, but the worst plague-infested areas were in the outlying districts of Whitechapel, Stepney, St Martin-in-the Fields and Westminster. In fact the plague was in decline by the time the fire broke out and this decline was happening all over Europe.

Next on the agenda of unpleasant illnesses that afflicted seventeenth-century England came Smallpox, which took over as soon as the plague disappeared. Smallpox was really a generic name for any type of skin eruption, from syphilis or chicken pox to measles or smallpox, but it mainly affected children. During the latter part of the century smallpox killed around 2000 people a year, and 80 per cent of those were children under twelve years of age. Smallpox wasn't as frightening as the plague simply because quite a lot of people survived it, and it was understood that once you'd had it you were then immune to the disease. They even had a rough idea about immunising children against it, as John Evelyn writes in his diary on September 15, 1685:

'Whilst supper was making ready I went and made a visit to Mrs Grahames...she was an excellent housewife, a prudent and vertuous Lady: Her eldest son, was now sick there of small pox, but in a likely way of recovery; and other of her childen ran about, and among the infected, which

she said she let them do on purpose that they might whilst young, passe that fatal disseace, which she fancied they were to undergo one time or other, and this would be the best.'

John Evelyn had recently lost two daughters from smallpox and so appreciated that a small dose of the disease would build up the body's immunity to it. Evelyn also makes some interesting observations of medical experiments and cures. On March 28, 1667 he writes:

'The Society experimented the transfusion of bloud, out of one animal into another; it was successfuly don out of a sheepe into a dog, 'til the sheepe died, the dog well, and was ordered to be carefully looked to...'

Five years later Evelyn witnessed a 'cruel operation' in which a sailor had a gangrenous leg amputated below the knee:

'The stout and gallent man, enduring it with incredible patience, and that without being bound to his chaire, as is usual in such painful operations, or hardly making a face or crying oh...The leg was so rotten and gangreen'd, that one might have run a straw through it... I do not remember that ever in my life I smelt so intollerable stink as what issu'd from the part was cut off.'

It's not too surprising to learn that the sailor died anyway.

Despite all the work going on at the time on anatomy, ancient practices such as blood letting (cupping) were still happening – even to such notables as Lord Berkeley and King Charles II. When Lord Berkeley *'fell downe in the Gallery at White-Hall of a fit of Apoplexie'* several famous doctors applied hot fire-pans and Spirit of Amber to his head, *'but nothing was found so effectual as cupping on the shoulders: an almost miraculous restauration.'* No doubt the fit abated because he was weak from losing so much blood. When King Charles suffered similar apoplectic fits his doctors spent five days letting blood before he died, and it seems probable that they bled the poor bloke to death.

A vast fund of medical knowledge and technique was built up during the seventeenth century but was kept in academic circles instead of being used for the benefit of common, or even royal, folk. The invention of the obstetric forceps is one such case. Dr William Chamberlen invented them, but kept his invention a strict secret – not even the women he delivered realised what he was up to. When he died the secret passed on to his son and his invention didn't come to light for 150 years. Given that doctors rarely let anyone else in on their secrets, it's hardly surprising that books along the lines of 'The Complete Home Doctor' appeared – *The Queen's Closet Opened* and *Culpeper's Pharmacopoeia Londinensis* being two examples.

As you will see in the following pages, they contain weird and wonderful concoctions which claim to cure all manner of loosely-defined ailments. Far be it from me to say that applying a mixture of honey, egg yolk, white dog's turd and frankincense to your piles isn't going to cure them, but I wouldn't put money on it (come to think of it, that would probably be just as effective). I wouldn't have thought that laying a turf of green grass on your navel is going to cure your colic, either, but you never can tell (Samuel Pepys thought he got colic from washing his feet and not doing up his waistcoat properly). Mind you, with the increasing interest in alternative medicine these days, it might just catch on. Next time your doctor's at a loss to know what to do about your gross humors, plague, bloody flux, consumption or ague, flick through the rest of this book, mix up the appropriate concoction and apply it to the affected place 'as hot as may be borne'.

Tom Isitt
August 1987

For a Sore Throat

Mingle burnt Allum, the yolk of an Egge, powder of White Dogs turd, and some Honey together, tye a clowt on the end of a stick wet in this mixture, and therewith rub the throat: or mixe white Dogs turd and Honey, spread it on Sheeps leather, and apply it to the Throat.

To make Childrens Teeth come without pain, Proved

Take the head of a Hare boyled or roasted, and with the brain thereof mingle Honey and Butter, and therewith anoynt the childs gums as often as you please.

Dr. Atkins Powder

Take Earthworms and slit them, and wash them with white Wine, then dry them in an Oven, and powder them, and put to every shilling weight of their powder, a groat weight of Ivory, and as much of Harts horn scraped and mingle them together, boyl in his broth Parsley roots and Fennel roots, and a little Nutmeg; if he will not take this, give him every morning two spoonfuls of Oxymel Compositum alone, or in Beer, or else burn some Juniper, and take one ounce of the ashes , and put in an Hypocras bag, with a quarter of a Nutmeg beaten, and run a pint of Rhenish Wine or white Wine through it four or five times, and let him every morning drink a draught of the Wine with Sugar.

A Medicine for the Worms

Take a little fresh Butter and Honey, melt it, and anoynt therewith the child
from the Stomach to the Navil, then take powder of Myrrhe and strew it
up-on the plàce so anoynted, cover it with a brown paper, and binde a cloth
over it, and so anoynt the child three nights one after the other. This Myrrhe
is also good to swallow in a morning for shortness of breath, and to chew it
in the month for Rhumes.

To make Hair grow thick

Take three spoonfulls of Honey, and a good handful of Vine sprigs that twist like wire, and beat them well, and strain their juyce into the Honey, and anoynt the bald places therewith.

For the Piles

Roast quick Snails in their shels, pick out their meat with a pin, and beat them in a Mortar with some powder of Pepper to a Salve, then take the dryed roots of Pilewort in powder, and strew it thin on the plaister, and apply it as hot as you can suffer it.

For Womens sore Paps or Breasts

Take Bean flower two handfulls, Wheaten Bran, and powder of Fenugreek of each one handfull, one pound of white Wine Vineger, three spoonfuls of Honey, three yolks of Egges, boyl all till they be very thick, and lay it warm to the Breast. This will both break and heal it. Crush out the matter when you change the plaister. Or take Oyl of Roses, Bean flower, and the yolk of an Egge with a little Vinegar, set it on the fire till it be luke warm and no more, then with a feather anoynt the sore places.

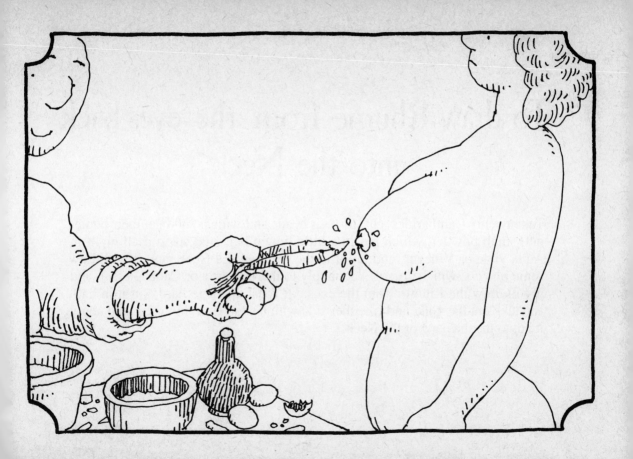

To draw Rhume from the eyes back into the Neck

Take twenty Cantharides, cut off their heads and wings, and beat their bodies into small powder, which put in a little linnen bag, and steep it all night in Aqua vitae or Vinegar, and lay it to the Nape of the Neck, and it will draw some blisters, which clip off, and apply to them an Ivie or Cabbage leaf, and it will draw the Rhume from the eyes. Or roast an Egge hard, cut it in half, and take out the yolk, and fil either side with beaten Cummin seed, and apply it hot to the the nape of the Neck.

For the Colick

Take half a sheet of white paper, anoynt it all over with Oyl Olive, and strew thereon gross Pepper, and so lay it to the belly from the Navil downward.

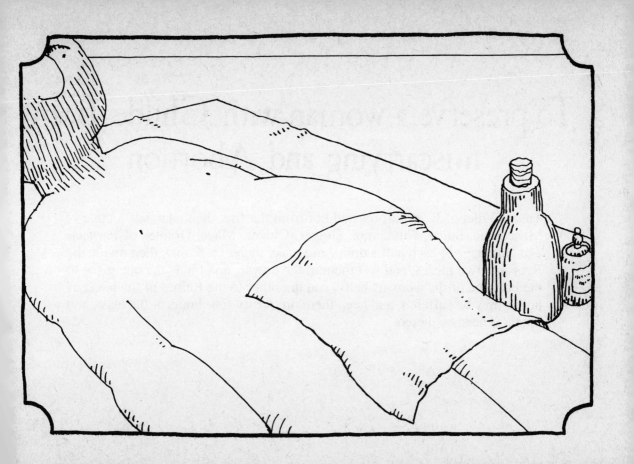

To preserve a woman with Childe from miscarrying and Abortion

Take a Fillet of Beef half roasted hot from the fire, then take half a pinte of Muscadine, Sugar, Cinnamon, Ginger, Cloves, Mace, Graines of Paradise and Nutmegs, of each half a dram, and make thereof a Sawce, then divide the Beef into two pieces, and wet them in the Sawce, and binde the one piece to the bottome of the womans belly, and the other to the Reines of the back, as hot as may be suffered, and keep them on twenty four hours at the least, and longer if need be thereof.

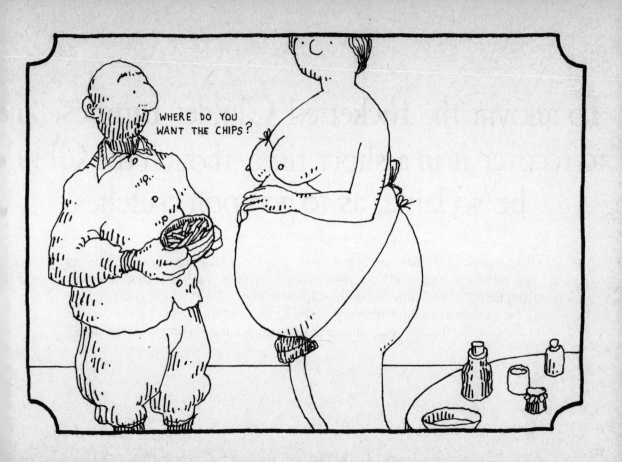

To anoynt the Ricketted Childes Limbes, and to recover it in a short time, though the Child be so lame, as to go upon crutches

Take a peck of Garden Snails and bruise them, put them into a course Canvas bag and hang it up, and set a dish under to receive the liquor that droppeth from them, wherewith anoynt the Childe in every Joynt which you perceive to be weak before the fire every morning and evening. This I have known made a childe that was extream weak to go alone, using it only a weeks time.

To procure Sleep

Bruise a handful of Aniseeds, and steep them in red Rose water, and make it up in little bags, and binde one of them to each Nosthril, and it will cause sleep.

For Worms in Children

Take three pound of Prunes, Sena one ounce and a half, sweet Fennel seed one ounce and a half, Rhubarb half an ounce, tie all these in a bag with a stone to it, and put them into a great quantity of water, then put the prunes on the top, and let it stew six or seven hours, till the liquor be even with the Prunes, so drink of the liquor two or three spoonfuls, and eat of the Prunes in the morning fasting, and at four a clock in the afternoon.

To cure a Shock Dog that hath the Mangie

Take four ounces of Tar, mixe it with some fresh Grease, so as it may run, then put to it some Brimstone powdered, halfe a spoonefull of Gunpowder powdered, and two spoonfuls of Honey, mixe them well, and therewith anoynt the Dog, in the summer time tie him in the hot Sun, that the Oyntment may soak into him, in the winter time lay him on thick fresh Hay, and there keep him that the heat of his body may heat and melt it. Thrice dressing it will cure him.

A Plaister to cleer the Stomach and comfort it

Take a red Rose cake, and toast the upper side of it at the fire, stick it thick full of Cloves, and dip it in a little quantity of Aqua vitae and white Wine Vinegar warmed very hot in a chafing dish of coals, lay it to the Stomach as hot as can be suffered, and binde it fast on all night.

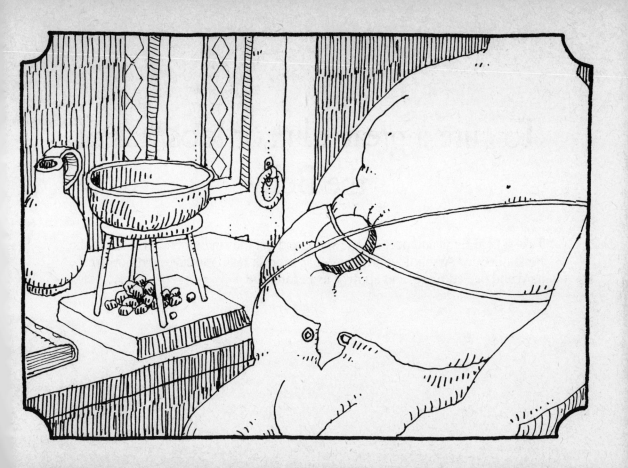

To cure a great Flux or loosness of the Belly

Take a hard Egge and peel off the shell, and put the smaller end of it hot to the Fundament or Arsehole, and when that is cold, take another such hot, fresh, hard and peeled Egge, and apply it as before said.

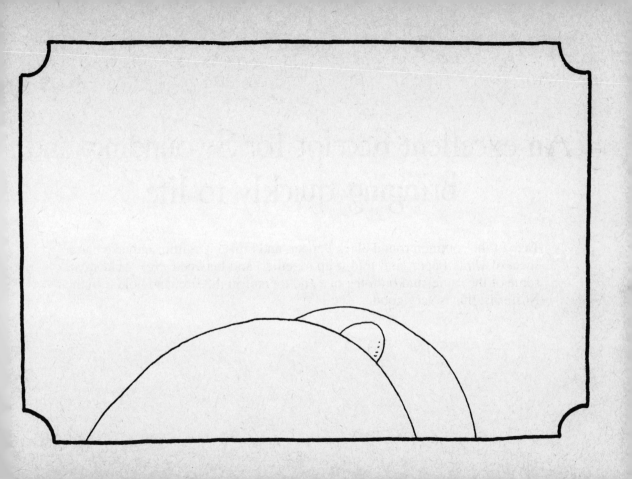

An excellent Receipt for Swounding, and bringing quickly to life

Take of the common round black Pepper, and bruise it a little, and take half a sheet of white Paper, and fold it up together, and between every fold strew some of the same, and burn the one end thereof in the fire, and hold it to the Nosthrils; this is very good.

Dr. Stevens for the Gowt. Proved

Take two pound of Virgins Waxe, of Boars grease half an ounce, of Sheeps Suet two ounces, of Neats foot Oyl two ounces, of Plantain and Rose water each two drams, of Spike water one dram, of Dragon water half an ounce, as much of Borage water, and Dr. Stevens water, two Nutmegs, twelve Cloves, and some Mace of the best, beat them small together, and put them into a pot, and boyl it over a soft fire, untill it become a Salve, then chafe the place where the party is grieved as hot as he may suffer, and then spread it on a fine linnen cloth, and lay it upon the place six or eight dayes.

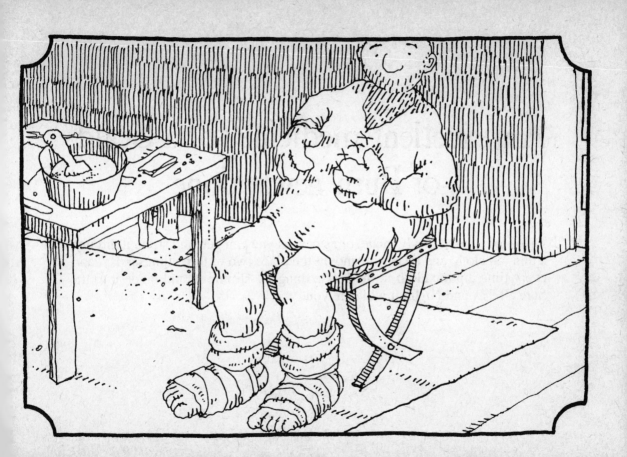

An excellent medicine for a Scald, or Burn newly done

Take Horse-dung newly made, or as new as you can get, and strain it through a thin old cloth, and therewith anoynt the place two or three times a day, and every time dip the cloth in the Horse dung, so straine it, and binde it to the Sore all Day and Night, it will cure you.

To make a Women have a Nipple that hath none, and would give suck

Take a Wicker bottle that hath a little mouth, and fill it full of hot water, and stop it close till the bottle be through hot, then let out the water, and set the mouth of the bottle close to the Nipple, as long as there is any heat in the bottle it will cleave fast.

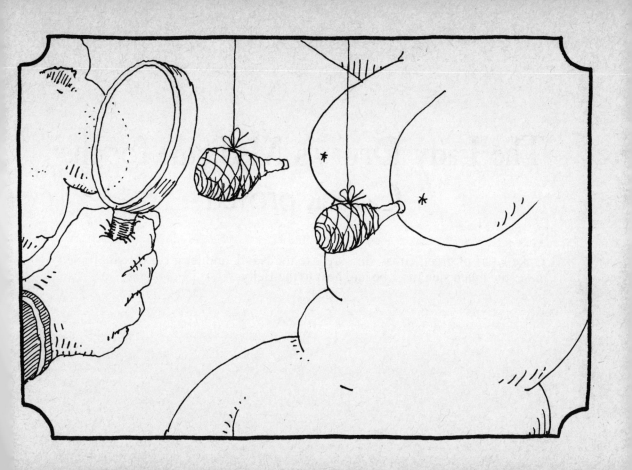

The Lady Drury's Medicine for the Colick proved

Take a turf of green Grass, and lay it to the Navil, and let it lye till you finde ease, the green side must be laid next to the Belly.

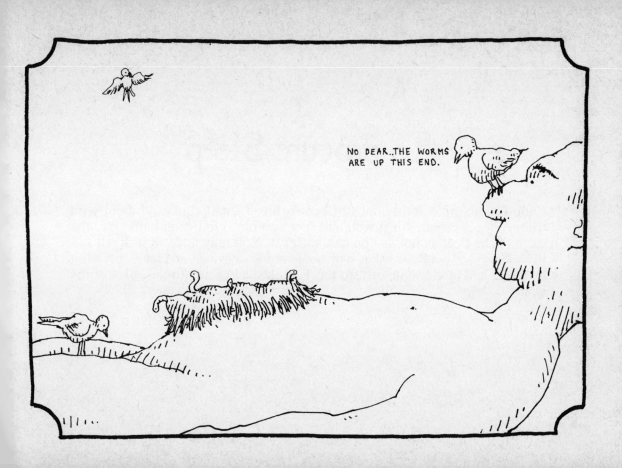

To procure Sleep

Chop Cammomile and crumbs of brown bread small, and boyl them with white Wine Vinegar, stir it well and spread it on a cloth, and binde it to the soles of the Feet as hot as you can suffer it. You may adde to it dryed red Rose leaves, or red Rose cakes with some red Rose water, and let it heat till it be thick, and binde some of it to the Temples, and some to the soles of the Feet.

The Bishop of Worcesters admirably curing Powder

Take black tips of Crabs claws when the Sun entrs into Cancer, which is every year on the eleventh day of June, pick and wash them clean, and beat them into fine powder, which finely searce, then take Musk and Civet, of each three grains, Ambergreese twelve grains, rub them in the bottom of the Mortar, and then beat them and the powder of the claws together; then with a pound of this powder mixe one ounce of the Magistery of Pearl. Then take ten skins of Adders, or Snakes, or Slow worms, cut them in pieces, and put them into a Pipkin to a pinte and half of Spring water, cover it close, and set it on a gentle fire to simper only, not to boyl, for ten or twelve hours, in which time it wil be turned into a Jelley, and therewith make the said powder into balls. If such skins are not to be gotten, then take six ounces of shaved Harts horn, and boyl it to a Jelley, and therewith make the said powder into bals; the horn must be of red Deer, kild in August when the Moon is in Leo, for that is best. The Dose is seven or eight grains in Beer or Wine.

A special water for Consumption

Take a peck of garden shell snails, wash them in small Beer, put them into a great Iron drippin pan, and set them on the hot fire of charcoals, and keep them constantly stirring till they make no noise at all, then with a knife and cloth pick them out, and wipe them clean, then bruise them in a stone Mortar, shels and all, then take a quart of Earth worms, rip them up with a knife, and scowr them with Salt, and wash them clean and beat them in the Mortar: Then take a large clean brass pot to distil them in, put into it two handfuls of Angelica, on them lay two handfuls of Celandine, a quart of Rosemary flowers, of Betony and Agrimony, of each two handfuls, Bears foot, red Dock leaves, the bark of Barberries and Wood Sorrel, of each one handful, Rice half a handful, Fenugreek and Turmerick, of each one ounce, Saffron dried and beaten into powder the weight of six pence, Harts horn and Cloves beaten, of each three ounces, when all these are in the pot, put the Snails and Worms upon them, and then pour on them three gallons of strong Ale; then set on the Limbeck and paste it close with Rye dough, that no ayr come out or get in, and so let it stand one and twenty hours', and distil it with a moderate fire, and receive the several quarts in several glasses close stopt. The Patient must take every morning fasting, and not sleep after it, two spoonfuls of the strongest water and four spoonfuls of the weakest at one time, fasting two hours after it.

A comfortable Juleb for a Feaver

Take Barley water and white Wine of each one pinte, Whey one quart, put to it two ounces of Conserve of Barberies, and the Juyces of two Limons and two Oranges. This will cool and open the body and comfort it. If the Feaver be extream hot, take two white salt Herrings, slit them down the back, and binde them to the soles of the feet for twelve hours. In want of Herrings take two Pigeons cut open, and so apply them.

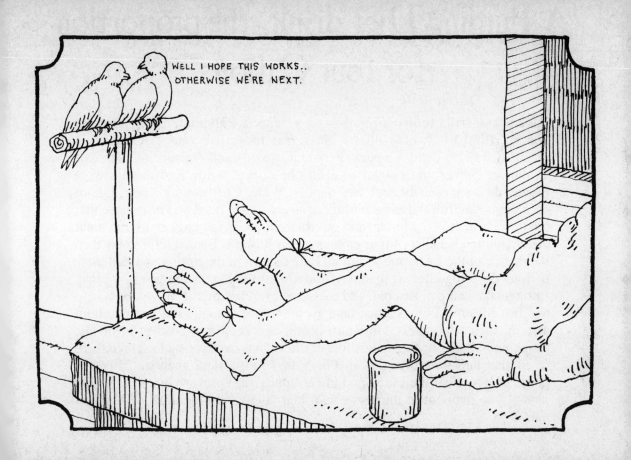

A Purging Diet drink, the proportion for four Gallons

Take Sarsaparilla four ounces, Sena six ounces, Polypodie of the Oak six ounces, Rhubarb twelve drams, Sassafras roots two ounces, Agarick I ounce, Sea Scurvy grass a peck, Fennel, Caroway and Aniseed of each half an ounce, Cloves and Ginger of each one ounce, wilde Radish and white Flower de Luce roots of each two ounces, Water Cresses and Brook-lime of each eight handfuls, slice such of these as are to be sliced and beat those that are to be beaten in a Mortar, and put them in a Canvas bag, and let it stand eight days in a Rundlet of four gallons of ten shillings Beer, a little lower then the middle of the Beer, and so tun it. Take thereof in the Spring and Fall three or four days together in manner following, every morning at six a clock fasting, take half a pinte cold, and use some exercise after it till you be warm, and fast till nine a clock, then take such another draught and fast one hour after it, then take some thin warm broth, and keep a good dyet at meals, eating no Sallades or flegmatick meats, after dinner at three a clock take there of another half pint: thus do for 3 or 4 days in the same manner. This will purge gently, clear the bloud and inward parts, and prevent diseases. If you please, you may put to the above said ingredients two handfuls of Mayden hair.

To take away Hair

Take the shels of fifty two Egges, beat them small, and still them with a good fire, and with the water anoint your self, where you would have the hair off: Or else Cats dung that is hard and dryed, beaten to powder, and tempered with strong Vinegar, and anoynted on the place.

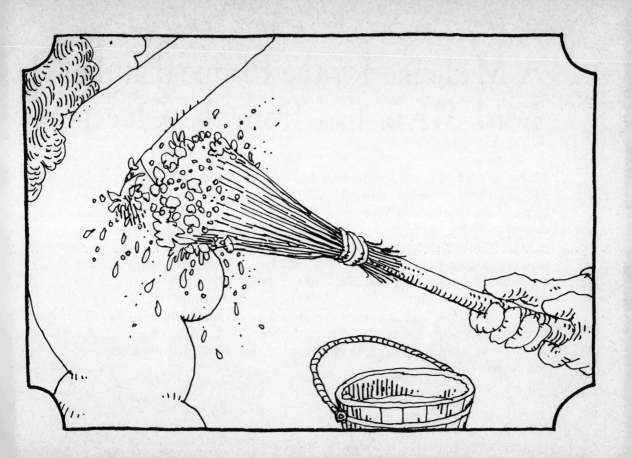

A Medicine for the Plague that the Lord Mayor had from the Queen

Take of Sage, Elder, and red Bramble leaves of each one little handful, stamp and strain them together, through a cloth with a quart of white Wine, then take a quantity of white Vinegar, and mingle all these together, and drink thereof morning and night a spoonful at a time nine days together, and you shall be whole: There is no Medicine more excellent then this, when the sore doth appear then to take a Cock Chick, and Pullet, and let the rump be bare, and hold the rump of the said Chick to the sore, and it will gape and labour for life, and in the end dye, then take another, and the third, and so long as any doe dye; for when the poyson is quite drawn out, the Chick will live, the sore presently will asswage and the party recover: Mr. Winlour proved this upon one of his own children, the thirteenth Chick dyed, the fourteenth lived and the party cured.

For the Piles

Take one spoonful of white Dogs turd, as much white Frankincense, and twenty four grains of Aloes, beat them fine and searce them, then take one spoonful of Honey, the yolk of an Egge, and as much oyl of Roses as will make it to an oyntment, mingle them well together, and anoynt the grieved place: if the sore be inward, wet a Tent of Lint in the Oyntment, and put it into the Fundament, and spread some of the Oyntments on a cloth, and put that on it. This is a present remedy.

To help deafnesse

Take a peece of Rye dough the bignesse of an Egge, and of that fashion, bake it dry in an Oven, cut off the end, and with a knife cut out the paste and make it hollow, then put into it a little Aqua Composita, and stir it, and so hot as you can endure it, apply it to the deaf ear till it be cold; you must keep your head very warm. If both ears be grieved, make two of them, and use those three times.